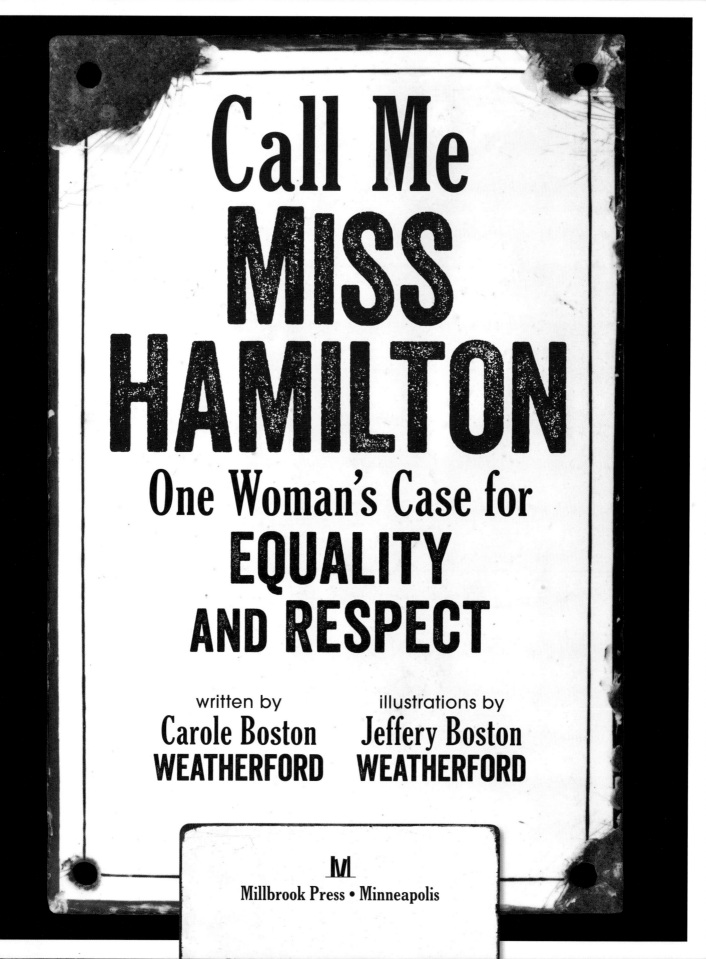

Call Me
MISS
HAMILTON

One Woman's Case for
EQUALITY
AND RESPECT

written by
Carole Boston
WEATHERFORD

illustrations by
Jeffery Boston
WEATHERFORD

M

Millbrook Press • Minneapolis

THIS MISS FIRST ANSWERED TO "MARY,"

the name that her parents,

Robert and Elizabeth Hamilton,

gave her in 1935.

Her name on their lips

was music to her ears.

Like her biblical namesake,

Mary, the mother of Jesus,

little Mary had a spirit within her.

It was a fighting spirit.

Mary's parents raised her

to know right from wrong.

In Catholic school, Mary admired her teachers.

Those nuns were tough and brave.

For a while, Mary wanted to be a nun;

to be called "Sister."

But she would find other ways

to bring about change.

She also knew Black from white.

Though African American, Mary's skin was so light she could have been mistaken for white.

Some of her relatives did pass for white, but not Mary.

SHE WAS PROUD TO BE BLACK!

Mary's family lived out west
where some states had outlawed
segregation. But African Americans
were still barred from many places
where white people could visit and shop and dine—
as were so-called "Indians" and "Mexicans."

After high school, Mary went east to college.
The all-girls school stressed scholarship,
manners, and charm. At receptions and teas,
addressing others by proper titles—

Miss, Mrs., or Mr.——
was a sign of
COURTESY
AND RESPECT.

After college,

she taught school in New York.

But her classroom

was not her only concern.

Mary cared about equal justice.

She cared about the Civil Rights Movement.

FOR HER, THE MOVEMENT MEANT

THAT BLACK PEOPLE WERE FINALLY FIGHTING BACK!

IN 1960, SHE JOINED THAT FIGHT.

As a member of CORE, the Congress of Racial Equality, Mary went on Freedom Rides.

Busloads of Black and white people

from the North risked

their lives to test a new court ruling

that outlawed segregation

on interstate buses and railroads.

Could Black passengers

really sit where they pleased?

Was the law worth

the paper it was

printed on?

Down south, the Freedom Riders' courage was tested.

They saw the color line with their own eyes.

In town after town: "colored" drinking fountains, restrooms, waiting rooms, and entrances; and whites-only restaurants, hotels, theaters, parks, and swimming pools.

COLORED

Sometimes, the protesters couldn't believe their ears.

Without so much as a second thought, whites called African Americans "out of their names," addressing grown men as "boy" and women as "girl" or "auntie," rather than **Miss, Mrs., or Mr.**

And African Americans were expected to answer.

Hecklers called the protesters even worse—
names too hateful to print.

In 1961, Mary was arrested in Mississippi.

In her mug shot, the sign around her neck

bears no name, only a number: 21068.

Again and again, Mary was arrested.

She told one jailer who threatened to harm her that she'd fight as if her life depended on it.

When another jailer trapped her in an elevator, she refused to scream, just for spite.

Despite beatings, she kept resisting.

Relying on nonviolence

TO PRESS FOR JUSTICE AND EQUALITY.

In the Civil Rights Movement, Mary was known for her *fiery spirit.*

That's why Martin Luther King Jr. gave her the nickname Red.

CORE

Wants a FAIR World

FREEDOM RIDE CORE

Her strong convictions led to her becoming the first woman to head CORE's southern region. Pledged to nonviolence, Mary could not stomach unfairness or disrespect.

In Tennessee, Mary was arrested again—
this time for picketing a theater
that made Black moviegoers sit in the balcony.
When the mayor came to the jail
and called her Mary, she demanded
that he call her "Miss Hamilton."

"IF YOU DON'T KNOW HOW TO SPEAK TO A LADY," she said, "THEN GET OUT OF MY CELL."

That wasn't the only time Mary was treated like she was second class due to her skin color.

In an Alabama court, a white prosecutor called her by her first name.

Mary refused to answer unless he called her "Miss Hamilton."

The judge ordered her to respond.

MARY REFUSED AGAIN.

The judge charged her with contempt of court
and threw her in jail.
Five days later, she got out
and refused to pay the fifty-dollar fine.

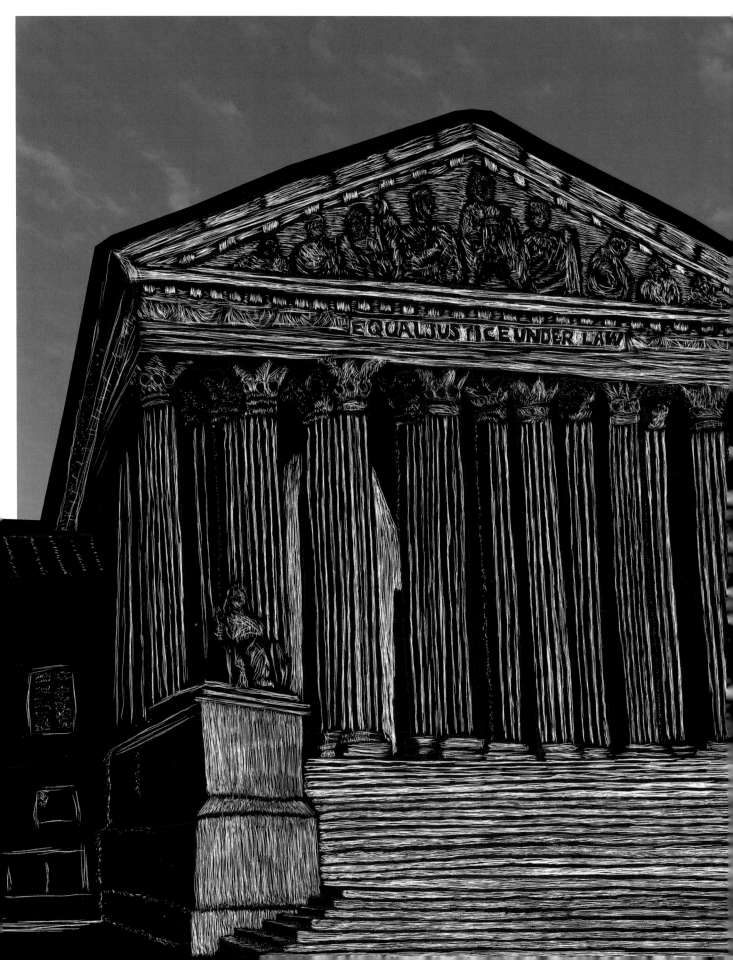

Mary had news for that judge.

She was not afraid to fight in court for what's right.

With NAACP lawyers on her side,

she fought the contempt charge all the way

to the United States Supreme Court.

In 1964, the highest court of the land
ruled in Mary's favor,
deciding that everyone in court
deserved respect.

MISS
HAMILTON
HAD
WON.

From then on, judges and lawyers addressed all African Americans in court

as Miss, Mrs., or Mr.—

the same as whites.

All because of the

"MISS MARY CASE."

WHAT'S IN A NAME?

Imagine being snatched from the continent of your birth, shipped across the ocean, stripped of your traditions, and then being grouped by skin color—black or Negro—rather than by tribe. Imagine being assigned a new name by a slave trader or slaveholder. Imagine having no last name at all and then when slavery ends being able to choose one for yourself and your family. Imagine white people never addressing you by your last name but by first name only—or worse. If you are a man, you are called "boy." If you are a woman, you are called "aunt." If you are lucky. Behind your back—or even to your face—you might be subjected to racial epithets. Even if you are grown, white children call you by your first name while addressing white adults with respect. And white adults never address you as "Miss," "Mrs.," or "Mr.," as you must address them.

For Mary Hamilton, that inequity was not just disrespectful; it was intolerable. That is why she took a brave stand. In court and in jail, she would not respond when addressed only by her first name.

Little is known about Mary's personal life or teaching career. However, her legacy of activism still resounds in courtrooms across the country. Because of the so-called "Miss Mary Case," all citizens are entitled not just to due process of law—fair treatment in the judicial system—but also to due respect, the right to be called Miss, Mrs., or Mr. in a court of law.

Mary Hamilton with CORE cofounder James Farmer

Timeline

1935: On October 13, Mary Lucille Hamilton is born to Robert Emerson DeCarlo and Elizabeth Winston Hamilton.

1937: On March 26, William H. Hastie is confirmed as the first Black federal judge in the Virgin Islands.

1939: Jane Bolin is appointed as the first African American woman judge in the United States on July 22.

1940: Thurgood Marshall leads the newly formed NAACP Legal Defense and Educational Fund.

1942: The Congress of Racial Equality (CORE) is founded in March.

1946: On June 3, the US Supreme Court rules in *Morgan v. Virginia* that segregation in interstate bus travel is unconstitutional.

1947: On April 10, Jackie Robinson of the Brooklyn Dodgers becomes the first African American to play Major League Baseball in the twentieth century.

1948: On May 3, the US Supreme Court rules that courts cannot enforce racially based discrimination in real estate contracts in *Shelley v. Kraemer*.

1953: Miss Hamilton graduates from East Denver High School.

1954: On May 17, the US Supreme Court rules that school segregation is unconstitutional in *Brown v. Board of Education of Topeka, Kansas*.

1955: On August 28, Emmett Till, a fourteen-year-old boy, is lynched while visiting Money, Mississippi.

Rosa Parks spearheads the modern Civil Rights Movement and the Montgomery Bus Boycott by refusing to give up her seat on a bus on December 1.

1956: On November 13, in *Browder v. Gayle*, the US Supreme Court affirms that bus segregation is unconstitutional under the Fourteenth Amendment.

1957: In January, the Southern Christian Leadership Conference (SCLC) is organized in Atlanta, Georgia.

In September, in Little Rock, Arkansas, nine African American students integrate Central High School.

1960: On February 1, four students from North Carolina Agricultural and Technical College stage a sit-in at Woolworth's whites-only lunch counter in Greensboro, sparking sit-ins across the country.

On May 6, the Civil Rights Act of 1960 outlaws voter suppression on the basis of race.

In March 1960, picketers outside the F.W. Woolworth store in Atlantic City, New Jersey, protest the chain's segregated lunch counters in the South. Woolworth's lunch counters were desegregated on July 25, 1960.

Members of the Washington Freedom Riders Committee hold protest signs out of bus windows in late May 1961.

Freedom Riders arrive in Montgomery, Alabama, on May 24, 1961, guarded by police and members of the National Guard.

In this April 1, 1964, photo, Mary Hamilton answers questions from reporters in her New Orleans office after the US Supreme Court decided in her favor.

1961: On May 4, the first Freedom Rides begin.

On June 26, while working with CORE, Miss Hamilton is arrested as a Freedom Rider in Jackson, Mississippi.

1963: In June, after hundreds of civil rights activists are arrested during protests in Gadsden, Alabama, Miss Hamilton refuses to answer the questions of a white prosecutor who addresses her by her first name.

On August 28, two hundred fifty thousand people participate in the March on Washington where Martin Luther King Jr. delivers his "I Have a Dream" speech.

On September 15, four girls are killed in the bombing of the 16th Street Baptist Church in Birmingham, Alabama.

1964: On March 30, in *Hamilton v. Alabama*, the Supreme Court rules that African Americans must be addressed with honorifics the same as whites.

On April 23, Miss Hamilton is featured on the front cover of *Jet* magazine for her legal victory.

On June 21, three civil rights workers are killed in Mississippi during Freedom Summer.

On July 2, the Civil Rights Act of 1964 is signed into law by President Lyndon B. Johnson.

1965: On February 21, Malcolm X is assassinated in Manhattan, New York.

On March 7, civil rights activists are assaulted by Alabama state troopers during the Selma to Montgomery March.

On August 6, the Voting Rights Act is signed into law by Johnson.

1966: In November, Constance Baker Motley becomes the first African American woman appointed to a federal judgeship.

1967: On October 2, Thurgood Marshall is sworn in as the first African American US Supreme Court justice.

1968: On April 4, Martin Luther King Jr. is assassinated in Memphis, Tennessee.

On April 11, the Civil Rights Act (Fair Housing Act) of 1968 is signed by Johnson.

In November, Shirley Chisholm is elected as the first African American woman to serve in the US Congress.

1971: Miss Hamilton earns her master of arts in teaching at Manhattanville College in Purchase, New York, and goes on to teach English at Sleepy Hollow High School.

On April 20, the Supreme Court rules in *Swann v. Charlotte-Mecklenburg Board of Education* that busing will be used as an effective means of integrating public schools.

1983: On November 2, Ronald Reagan signs a bill declaring Martin Luther King Day a federal holiday.

1990: Miss Hamilton retires from teaching.

2002: On November 11, Miss Hamilton dies from cancer at the age of sixty-seven.

Further Reading

Brimner, Larry Dane. *Twelve Days in May: Freedom Ride 1961.* Honesdale, PA: Calkins Creek, 2017.

Giovanni, Nikki. *Rosa.* Illustrated by Bryan Collier. New York: Henry Holt, 2005.

Lewis, John, and Andrew Aydin. March trilogy. Illustrated by Nate Powell. Marietta, GA: Top Shelf, 2013–2016.

Ramsey, Calvin Alexander, and Gwen Strauss. *Ruth and the Green Book.* Illustrated by Floyd Cooper. Minneapolis: Carolrhoda, 2010.

Rappaport, Doreen. *Martin's Big Words.* Illustrated by Bryan Collier. New York: Hyperion, 2007.

Weatherford, Carole Boston. *Be a King: Dr. Martin Luther King Jr.'s Dream and You.* Illustrated by James Ransome. New York: Bloomsbury, 2018.

Weatherford, Carole Boston. *Birmingham, 1963.* Honesdale, PA: Wordsong, 2007.

Weatherford, Carole Boston. *Freedom on the Menu: The Greensboro Sit-Ins.* Illustrated by Jerome Lagarrigue. New York: Dial, 2005.

For anyone who has ever been called "out of their name."
You have a right to demand respect!
—C.B.W.

For my mother, who has always stood tall in the face of
adversity and demanded the respect she deserves; and
my Bre'Anna who is always by my side rooting for me.
—J.B.W.

Millbrook Press™
An imprint of Lerner Publishing Group, Inc.
241 First Avenue North
Minneapolis, MN 55401 USA

For reading levels and more information, look up this title at www.lernerbooks.com.

Image credits: Library of Congress, pp. 5, 6, 7, 8, 12, 14, 19, 24, 26, 28; Duane Howell/The Denver Post/Getty Images, p. 36; AP Photo, pp. 37, 38 (bottom); AP Photo/Perry Aycock, p. 38 (middle); Everett Collection Historical/Alamy Stock Photo, p. 38 (top). Design elements: Harun Ozmen/Shutterstock.com; titelio/Shutterstock.com; irin-k/Shutterstock.com.
Jacket images: Harun Ozmen/Shutterstock.com; Library of Congress.

Main body text set in ITC Avant Garde Gothic Std. Typeface provided by Adobe Systems.
The illustrations in this book were rendered on scratchboard.

Library of Congress Cataloging-in-Publication Data

Names: Weatherford, Carole Boston, 1956- author. | Weatherford, Jeffery Boston, illustrator.
Title: Call me Miss Hamilton : one woman's case for equality and respect / Carole Boston Weatherford, Jeffery Boston Weatherford.
Description: Minneapolis : Millbrook Press, 2022. | Audience: Ages 7–11 | Audience: Grades 2–3 | Summary: "This picture book biography in verse tells the story of Mary Hamilton, an African American woman and Civil Rights activist, who was found to be in contempt of court when she would not respond to questions from an Alabama judge who used only her first name, while calling white people "Mr.," "Mrs.," or "Miss." The NAACP took her case, which appealed all the way to the US Supreme Court, which ruled in Mary Hamilton's favor." —Provided by publisher.
Identifiers: LCCN 2019039716 (print) | LCCN 2019039717 (ebook) | ISBN 9781541560406 (library binding) | ISBN 9781541599369 (ebook)
Subjects: LCSH: Hamilton, Mary Lucille, 1935–2002—Trials, litigation, etc.—Juvenile literature. | African American women civil rights workers—Alabama—Biography—Juvenile literature. | Civil rights workers—Alabama—Biography—Juvenile literature. | African Americans—Civil rights—Alabama—Juvenile literature. | Contempt of court—Alabama—Juvenile literature. | Alabama—Race relations—Juvenile literature. | Race discrimination—Law and legislation—Alabama—Juvenile literature. | Race discrimination—Law and legislation—United States—Juvenile literature. | Equality before the law—United States—Juvenile literature.
Classification: LCC KF224.H2425 W43 2022 (print) | LCC KF224.H2425 (ebook) | DDC 323.092 (B)—dc23

LC record available at https://lccn.loc.gov/2019039716
LC ebook record available at https://lccn.loc.gov/2019039717

Manufactured in the United States of America
1-46302-47173-7/19/2021